THE UNIVERSITY OF FLORIDA

Palm and Pine

Photography by Ray Carson and Kristen Bartlett Grace

Foreword by George E. Edmondson, Jr., aka Mr. Two Bits

Published by

dsa
Publishing & Design Inc.

203 W. Belmont Drive
Allen, Texas 75013
972-747-7866
FAX 972-747-0226
www.dsapubs.com

Publisher: Duff Tussing

Associate Publisher: Steve Boston

Photography: Ray Carson and Kristen Bartlett Grace

Additional Photography: Mary Warrick; *pg 65 (classroom) and pg 75 (student gathering)*

Design: Donnie Jones, The Press Group

All images in this book have been reproduced with the knowledge and prior consent of the photographers and no responsibility is accepted by the producer, publisher, or printer for any infringement of copyright or otherwise arising from the contents of this publication. Every effort has been made to ensure that credits accurately comply with the information supplied.

Printed in the US

PUBLISHER'S DATA

The University of Florida - Palm and Pine

Library of Congress Control Number: 2008901081

ISBN Number: 978-0-9774451-9-6

First Printing 2008

10 9 8 7 6 5 4 3 2 1

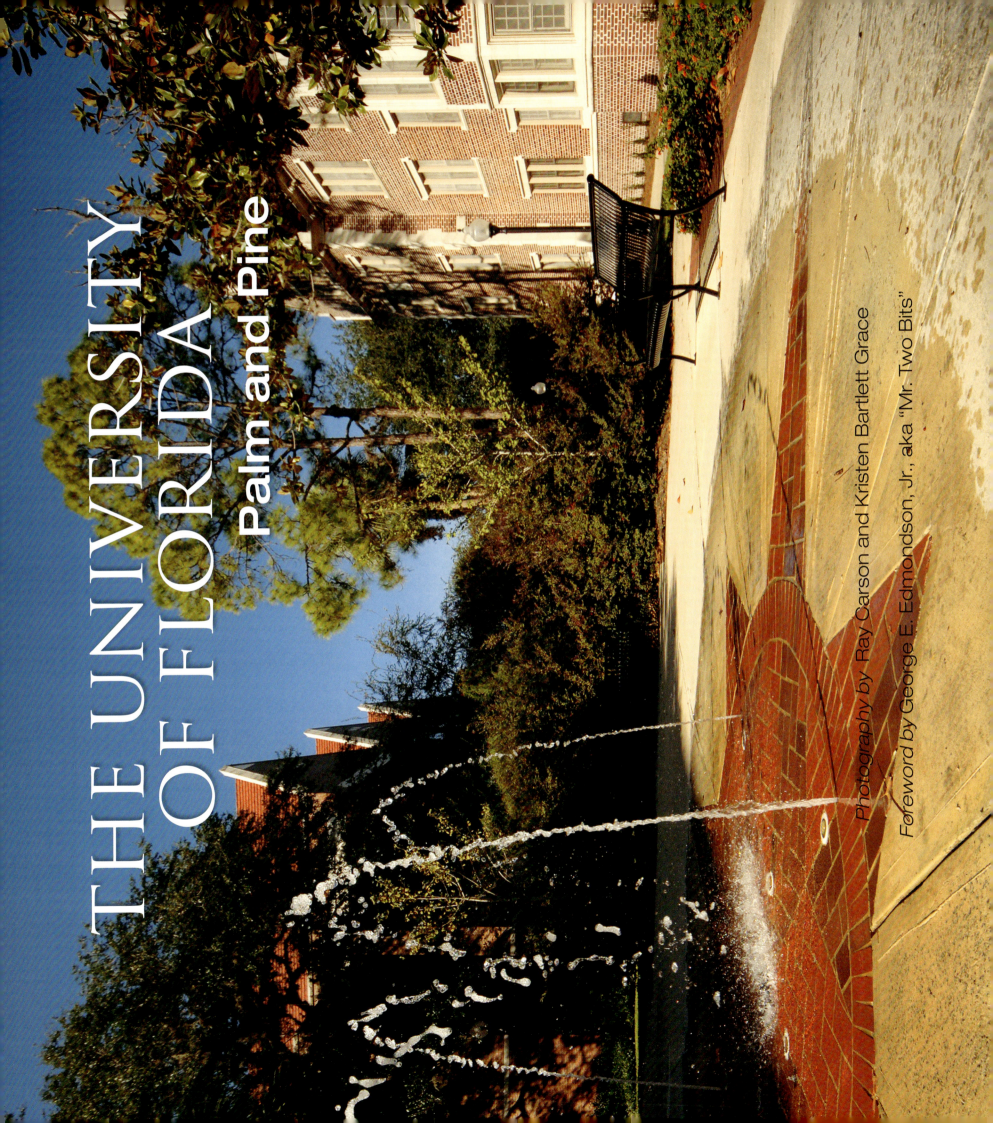

THE UNIVERSITY OF FLORIDA

Palm and Pine

Photography by Ray Carson and Kristen Bartlett Grace

Foreword by George E. Edmondson, Jr., aka "Mr. Two Bits"

Dear Gator alumni, fans and friends,

As I reflect on my memories of being a Gator, I think about the carillon bells ringing on a sunny day as students stroll through campus. I think of the energetic sensation that washes over the fans when the Gators take the field to play football in The Swamp. I think of the vine that is draped over and around the brick walls of our academic buildings. I think of the times when we celebrated our accomplishments together as a nation, as The Gator Nation®. I think of days to come, when we'll surely celebrate together again. I think of the promise this University has for our students, our communities, our state, our world. I think of the innovations, the cures, the companies and all of the wonderful things Gators have to offer the universe. As I think about what it means to be a Gator, I am overcome with gratitude. I am grateful to UF for so many things — it has been a place for me to live, to visit, to reunite. It is a bond — one that we are all touched by in a way only members of The Gator Nation® can understand.

As you flip through these pages and take in the beauty of our campus, it is my hope that the images will bring back wonderful memories of a place we all cherish. The sections are designed to tell a story — the story of a picturesque campus, passionate students, world-renowned academics, storied athletics and a vibrant community. I hope you'll keep this book on display in your home and enjoy it time and time again. It is my great honor to be a Gator and share this wonderful keepsake with you.

All Strong for Old Florida,

George E. Edmondson, Jr.
"Mr. Two Bits"

THE ASSOCIATION

The University of Florida Alumni Association...
Connecting The Gator Nation® since 1906

It was in 1906 that the University of Florida Alumni Association was born with a membership of fourteen young men. Since then, we have grown and now boast more than 55,000 members worldwide. While the volume of members has increased over the years — our mission remains the same: to foster and enhance the relationship between the University of Florida, its alumni, students and friends; and to support the University's mission of teaching, research and service.

Membership

- 55,000+ members
- Member benefits include discounts on restaurants, Gator merchandise, hotels, rental cars and much more
- Members receive the *UF Today* alumni magazine quarterly
- Members automatically become members of their local Gator Club®
- Membership dues directly support UF through student scholarships, programming and events

Recognition

The UF Alumni Association presents awards recognizing faculty, students and alumni for their outstanding contributions to UF:

- Distinguished Alumni Professor
- Outstanding Student Leaders & Scholars
- Distinguished Alumnus
- Young Alumni Awards
- Outstanding Gator Club® Leader Awards

Gator Clubs

Gator Clubs® are affiliated organizations of the UF Alumni Association and exist to support the mission of both the Alumni Association and the University of Florida. Gator Club activities include:

- Funding scholarships (Gator Clubs® have endowed more than $2.16 million in academic scholarships)
- Conducting International Gator Day community service projects
- Hosting local university and athletic functions

Special Events

The UF Alumni Association connects alumni and friends to UF through events and programming that celebrate the university. Annual events include:

- **Gator Nation Tailgate** — three hours before kickoff of each home game, the UFAA hosts the best tailgate party in town at Emerson Alumni Hall. These events are held at away games as well
- **Grand Guard 50-year Reunion** — held during football season, those who graduated 50 years ago are invited to this event and to be inducted into the Grand Guard
- **Spring Weekend** — Gators head back to Gainesville for a weekend of fun, football and fellowship. It includes entertainment, a BBQ and the Orange and Blue scrimmage
- **Silver Society** — this new tradition is a 25th reunion event and held during Spring Weekend
- **Back-to-College** — usually held in February, this event allows Gators to come "back to college" and learn about various fields studied on campus
- **Grad Bash** — held in Fall and Spring, this event honors graduating seniors with a party at Emerson Alumni Hall

Outreach

The OUTREACH program brings leading UF faculty and administrators to communities around the country to share their expertise and carry the university's message to alumni and friends. Gator Clubs® and other organizations can hear UF's leading researchers and faculty members in education, science and dozens of other fields in their own local area. Speakers have included the UF President, college deans and other notable faculty. In addition, the program includes a Gainesville component through the Phil Griffin Distinguished Lecture Series at Emerson Alumni Hall.

Student Alumni Association and the Florida Cicerones

The Student Alumni Association (SAA) falls under the umbrella of the UF Alumni Association and offers local discounts, career networking and social events for UF students. The SAA also produces the *F Book*, which is given to all incoming freshmen. This book educates students on the university, current and lost traditions and what it means to be a Gator. It also lists over 50 traditions to complete before graduation. By doing this, they become a UF TK (UF Tradition Keeper).

The Florida Cicerones are a group of approximately 150 students who serve as the official ambassadors for the University of Florida. They sponsor and plan programs for current and prospective UF students, alumni and members of the community. Their activities involve giving campus tours, hosting alumni and presidential events.

CONTENTS

THE UNIVERSITY OF FLORIDA

the campus

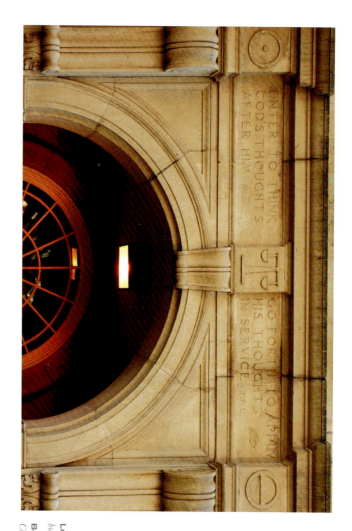

Left *Leigh Hall was built in 1927 and is part of a complex of buildings devoted to chemistry research and education.*
Below *The Florida Gym opened in 1949 and is home to the College of Health and Human Performance.*

Below *The UF Bookstore and Welcome Center opened in the summer of 2003.*

Above *The Fountain is located at the main entrance of the University of Florida next to Tigert Hall.*

Right *Smathers Library.*

Facing Page *Anderson Hall was originally known as "Language Hall."*

Above *Known as "Water Sculpture," this artwork is located at the College of Fine Arts.*

Facing Page *Located in Peabody Courtyard, this is a tribute to President Albert Murphree, who served from 1909–1927.*

Above *A classic shot of Century Tower and the University Auditorium, two of UF's most well-known buildings.*

Above *An evening shot of Emerson Alumni Hall.*

Facing Page *The Stephen C. O'Connell Center, also known as "The O'Dome", was named for former UF President Stephen C. O'Connell, who served from 1967 to 1973.*

Left *The Lady of Learning is located on the east side of Norman Hall, home to the College of Education.*

Below *Norman Hall was opened in 1934 as the P.K. Yonge Laboratory School for K - 12. It is rumored to be haunted.*

Above *Fall foliage at the University of Florida.*

Left *The Baughman Center on Lake Alice.*
Facing Page *Formerly known as the Women's Gymnasium, Kathryn Chicone Ustler Hall is home to the Center for Women's Studies and Gender Research.*

Right *Entrance of Smathers Library East.*

Facing Page *Interior of the University Auditorium.*

Left *The UF Orthopaedics and Sports Medicine institute opened to the public in 2004.*

Facing Page *Ben Hill Griffin Stadium*

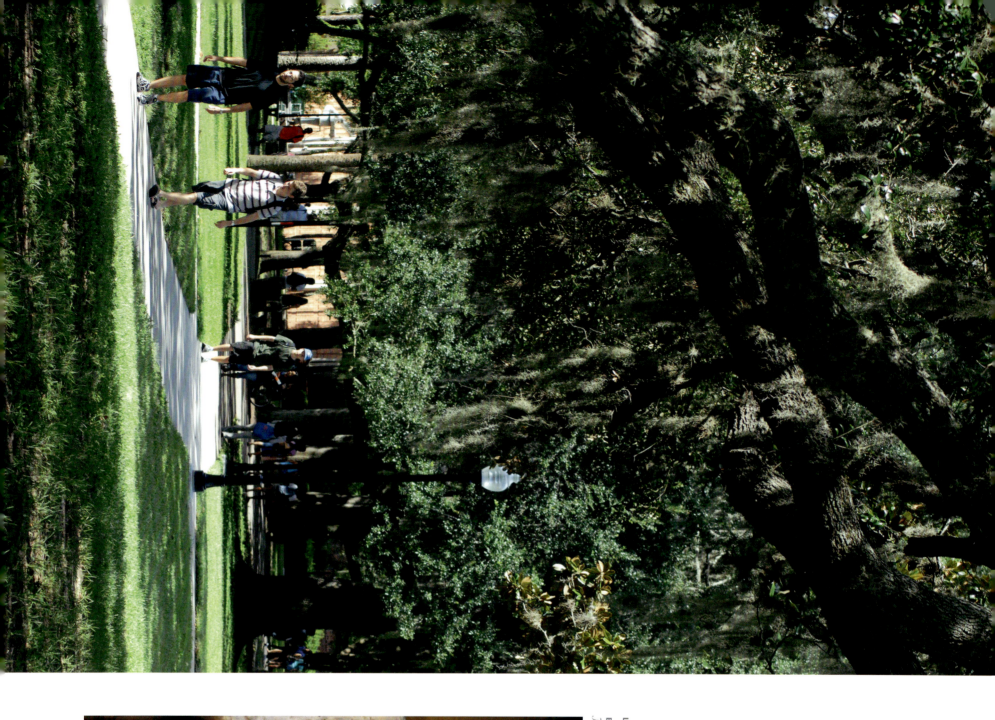

Left *One of many large oak trees on UT's campus at Union Lawn.*

Below *A close-up of "Media's People" located at the College of Journalism and Communications at Weimer Hall.*

Above *A student strolls through Peabody Courtyard.*

Below *Sheild Hall Courtyard: carved reliefs along the façade depict scenes of Florida's Spanish heritage and other themes. This entrance with the ship and the explorer is called the Macazo Tower.*

Left *McKnight Brain Institute.*

Right *This sculpture is known as "Balance" and is located in the HPNP Courtyard.*

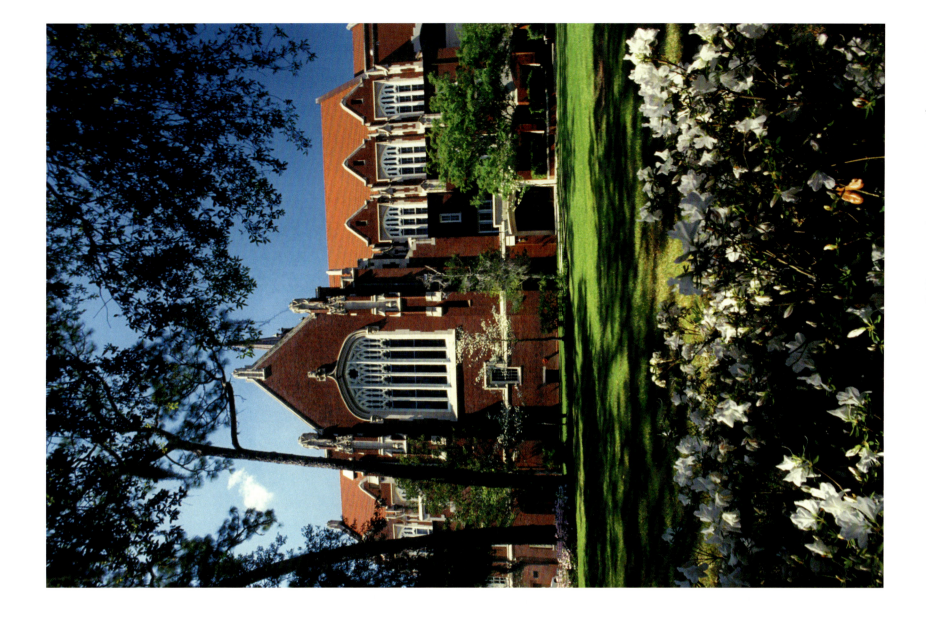

Facing Page *Green Pond at Reitz Union.*

Right *Azaleas in bloom near the University Auditorium.*

Below *Griffin-Floyd Hall.*

Above *The Baughman Center by day ...*

Above ...*and by night.*

Above *Turtle swimming in Green Pond.*

Facing Page *Graham Pond.*

Above *From an aerial view, four dorms actually spell UF. The dorms are Sledd, Thomas, Fletcher and Buckman.*

Facing Page *Commonly known as the "French Fries," this sculpture is actually titled "Alachua" and was installed in 1988.*

Above *Opened in 1913, Peabody Hall housed the teacher's college that would later become the College of Education.*

Right *A view of Century Tower through CSE (Computer Science and Engineering).*

Below *Wilmont Gardens, a historic campus garden known for its camellias.*

Facing Page *Azaleas in bloom near the UF Infirmary.*

Right *University Seal.*

Below *Vine-clad walls of Walker Hall, built in 1927.*

Left and Below *Lake Alice*

Above *Bats fly out of the Bat House in the evening during warm weather.*

Right *The Bat House is located across from Lake Alice.*

Above *The Phillips Center for the Performing Arts.*

Above *The Harn Museum of Art.*

Above *Opened in the fall of 1906, Buckman Hall was one of the first two original buildings on campus.*

Right *UF Bookstore and Welcome Center on Museum Road.*

THE UNIVERSITY OF FLORIDA

the students

Above *Staircell at the Reitz Union.*

Above *Broward Outdoor Recreation Complex.*
Left *Students studying in the new HUB.*

Above *A student prepares to give a vocal performance at the President's House.*

Left *University Auditorium.*

Above *Plaza of the Americas.*

Left *Converging sidewalks at the Plaza of the Americas.*

Right *Student running the steps of Ben Hill Griffin Stadium.*

Left *Gator Pond, across from Little Hall.*

Above *Professor lecturing a class.*
Left *New Engineering Building.*
Below *Terrace at Green Pond, Reitz Union.*

Above *Playing Four Square in Turlington Plaza.*

Right *Drama students during a Shakespearean Improv Class.*

Above *A performance at the McGuire Pavilion.*
Left *Getting some work done outside of Anderson Hall.*

Above *Walkway by Reitz Union.*

Above *A flurry of activity at the UF Bookstore and Welcome Center.*

Right *Aerial view of students at the College of Architecture.*

Below *New Library West.*

Above *Students taking time to break-dance on the Union Lawn.*
Left *Studying on the Plaza of the Americas.*
Facing Page *University Orchestra performance at the Phillips Center for the Performing Arts.*

Above *Little Courtyard.*

Above *For years, UF students have enjoyed various recreational activities at Lake Wauberg*

Right *Students gather at the Communicore Building*

THE UNIVERSITY OF FLORIDA
athletics

Above *Members of the Gators Soccer Team.*

Left *Stumpy Harris, UF alumnus, shows his Gator pride.*

Above *The statue of Albert and Alberta, located in the plaza at Emerson Alumni Hall, is a popular spot for photo opportunities.*

Above *The Pride of the Sunshine Fightin' Gator Marching Band.*

Right *Young Gator fans doing the chomp.*

Facing Page *More than 90,000 fans pack Ben Hill Griffin Stadium to watch Gator football every fall.*

Above *UF Men's Tennis.*

Right *UF Women's Diving.*

Below *Gator Volleyball.*

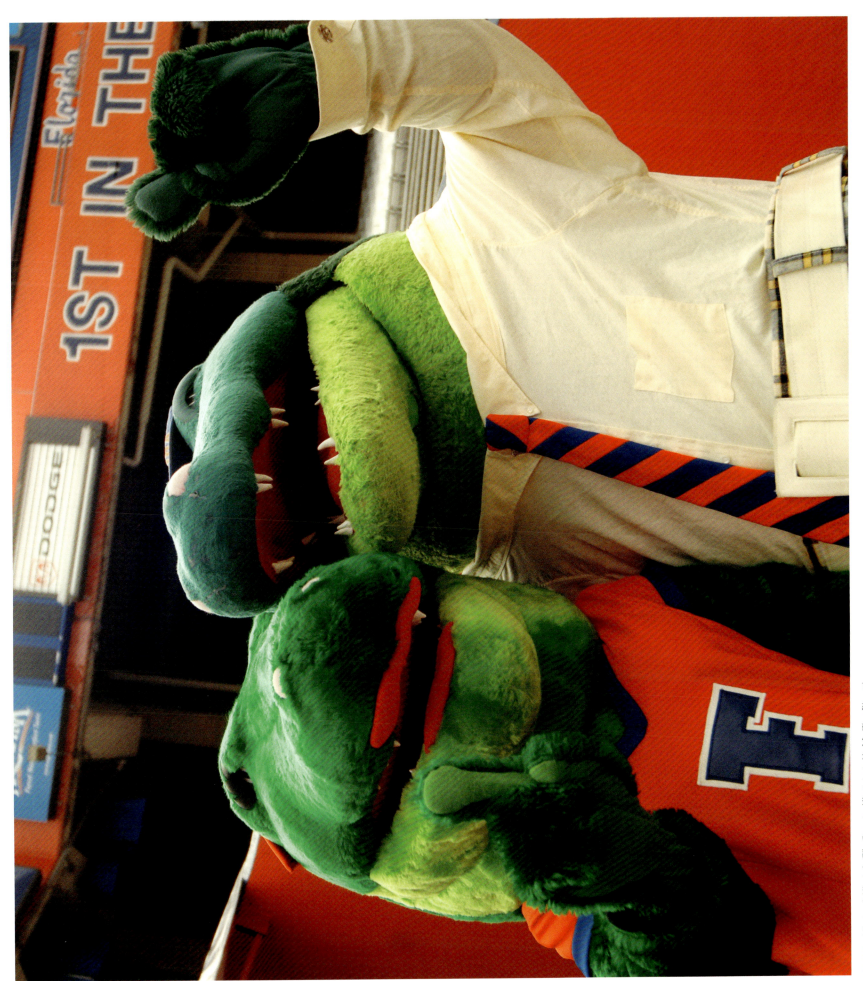

Above *Albert and Alberta in The Swamp; Albert sports his Mr. Two Bits attire.*

Above *A Gator family watches the homecoming parade.*

Right *Gator Fever is contagious!*

Right *The student section at UF basketball games is known as the "Rowdy Reptiles."*

Below *A UF gymnast competes in the O'Dome.*

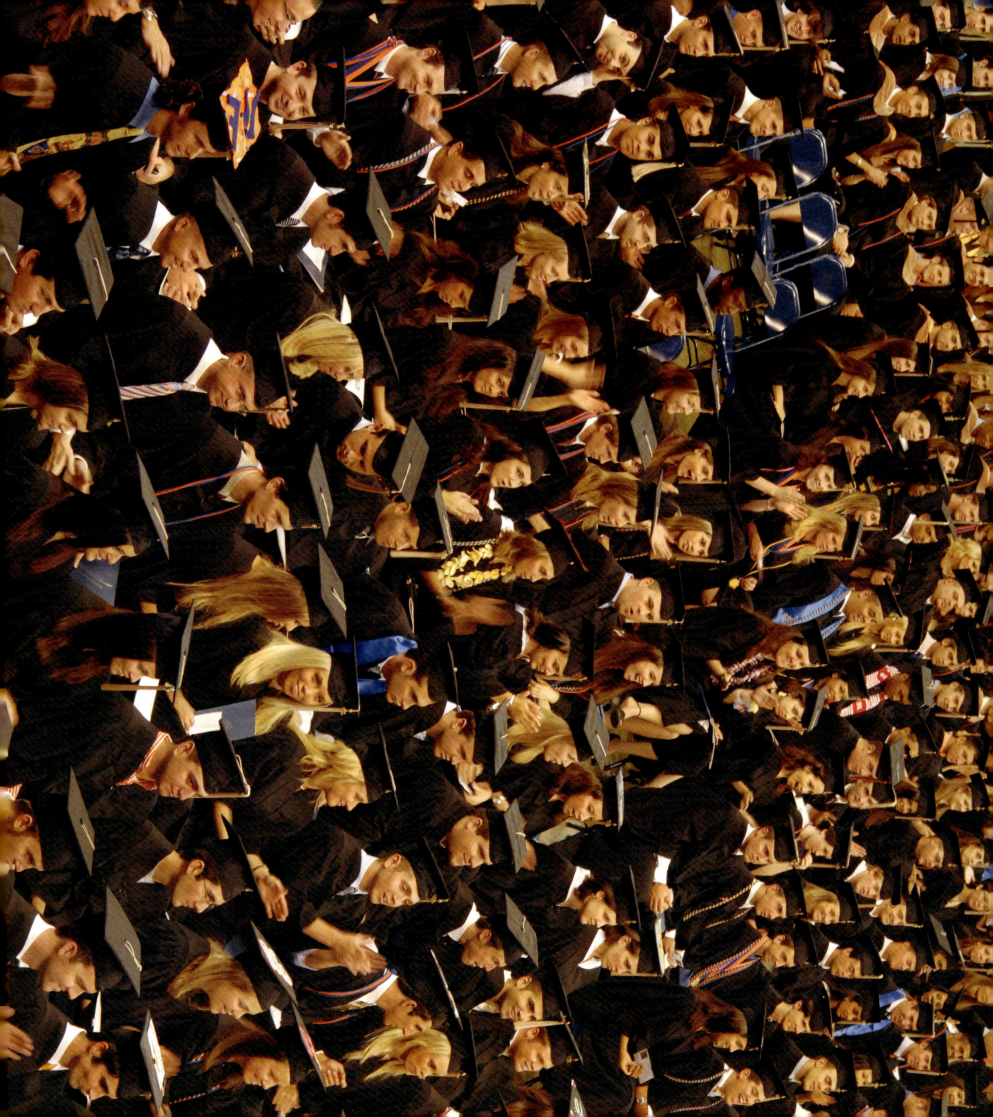

academics

THE UNIVERSITY OF FLORIDA

Above *The white coat ceremony symbolizes a student's entry into clinical study.*
Right *New Teaching Lab at the Orthopaedics and Sports Medicine Institute.*

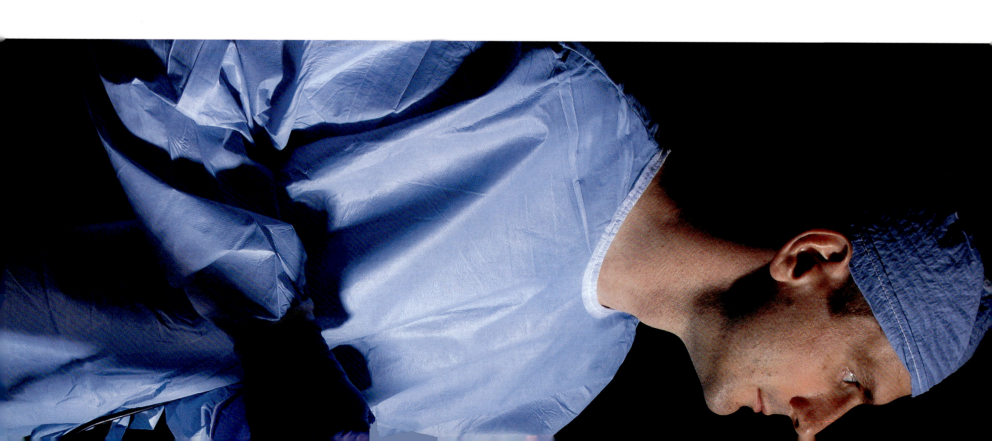

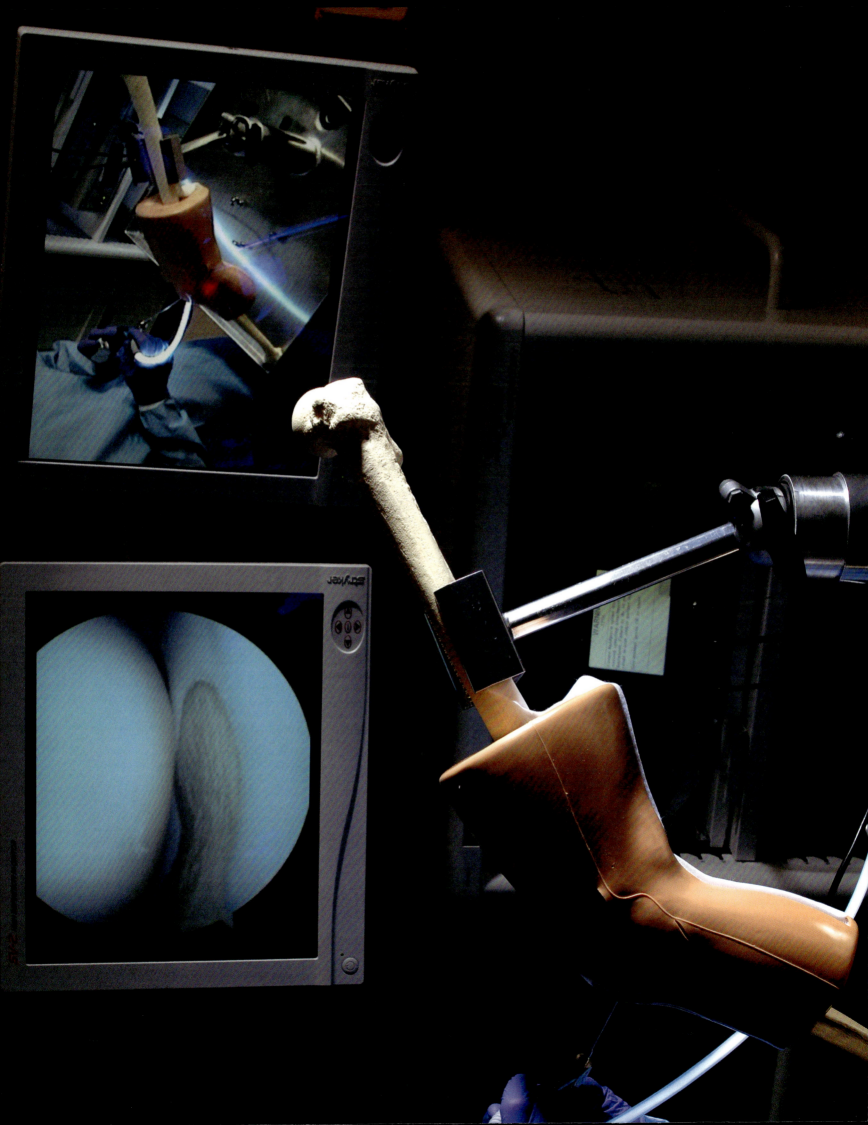

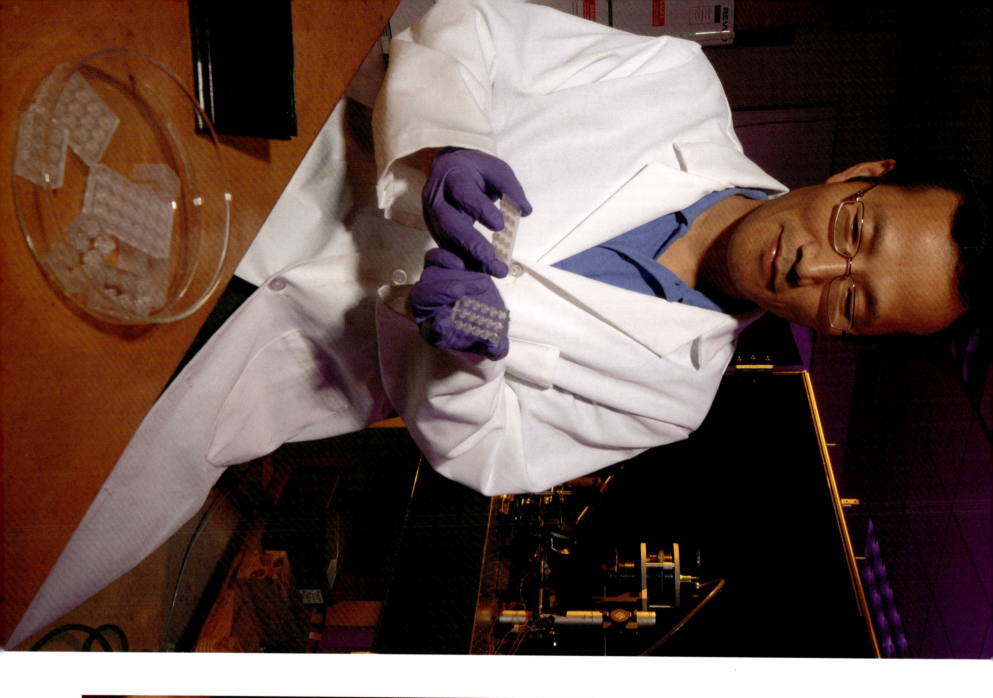

Left UF labs, like this one for engineering, are a constant source of innovation.

Below UF holds a number of graduation ceremonies each fall, spring and summer.

Above *A student drawing with charcoal in a Fine Arts course.*

PRESENTED IN HONOR OF THE 1996 NATIONAL FOOTBALL CHAMPIONSHIP
BY
WARREN M. CASON, GORDON H. "STUMPY" HARRIS AND JEFFREY A. ULMER
DEDICATED THIS DAY, APRIL 4, 1998

COURTYARD
OF CHAMPIONS

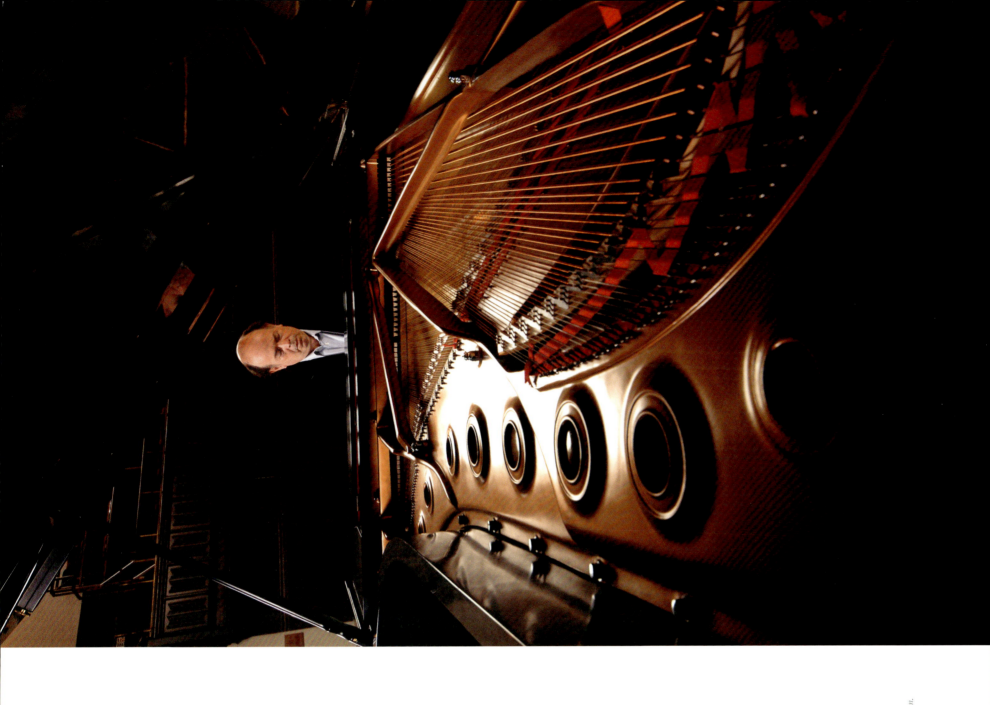

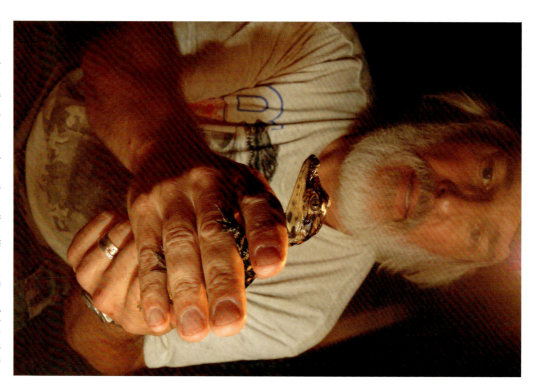

Above *As part of graduate research, a professor collects alligators at Orange Lake (south of Gainesville).*

Left *A lecture at the College of Education.*

Above *Virtual Reality Classroom.*

Left *Students gather to study outside of Norman Hall.*

Above *Butterfly release at the McGuire Center for Lepidoptera and Biodiversity.*
Right *Orthopaedics and Sports Medicine Institute.*

Above *Students at the White Coat Ceremony.*

SOCRATES
PLATO
ARISTOTLE
CONFUCIUS
QUINTILIAN
DA FELTRE
MELANCHTHON
LOYOLA
COMENIUS
PESTALOZZI
HERBART
FROEBEL
McGUFFEY
HORACE MANN
ELIOT

Right *Norman Hall.*

Below *A student throws a pot in a Fine Arts class.*

community

THE UNIVERSITY OF FLORIDA

Left *The Clock Tower in downtown Gainesville contains a clock that was built in 1885 and originally sat atop the old courthouse.*

Above *Prior to becoming the Hippodrome State Theatre, this building has served as the Courthouse, Federal Building and Post Office.*

Right *The Downtown Community Plaza is home to the Farmers Market each week in Gainesville.*

Above *University Avenue at night.*

Right *Gator Plaza.*

Facing Page *The Swamp, a popular establishment for students, alumni and fans.*

Above *Sand Hill Cranes at the Beef Teaching Unit.*

Left *Fall leaves and Spanish moss.*

Above *Paynes Prairie.*
Right *Juvenile alligator.*
Far Right *American Lotus.*

Above *The sun rising over Lake Alice.*

Left *Old Florida homestead west of Micanopy.*

Above *A wild azalea at Ginnroot Swamp.*

Left *Kanapaha Park on Tower Road.*

Above *Pine Cone at Kanapaha Park.*

Above *Poe Springs at the Santa Fe River.*

Right *A family of turtles swimming in the Santa Fe River.*

Above *New River.*

Above *Road sign on I-75 North.*